HANDY
LITTLE
GUIDE

Prayer

Barb Szyszkiewicz, OFS

Our Sunday Visitor
Huntington, Indiana

Nihil Obstat
Msgr. Michael Heintz, Ph.D.
Censor Librorum

Imprimatur
✠ Kevin C. Rhoades
Bishop of Fort Wayne-South Bend
December 19, 2020

The *Nihil Obstat* and *Imprimatur* are official declarations that a
book is free from doctrinal or moral error. It is not implied that
those who have granted the *Nihil Obstat* and *Imprimatur* agree with
the contents, opinions, or statements expressed.

Our Sunday Visitor Publishing Division
Our Sunday Visitor, Inc.
200 Noll Plaza
Huntington, IN 46750
1-800-348-2440

ISBN: 978-1-68192-694-0 (Inventory No. T2570)
LCCN: 2021930122

Cover and interior design: Amanda Falk
Cover and interior art: AdobeStock

PRINTED IN THE UNITED STATES OF AMERICA

Contents

Introduction
Why Pray?

God knows what's in our minds and on our hearts, as we learn in Psalm 44:21, but we have a very human need to verbalize that. Sharing our hearts and our feelings with others we trust deepens our relationship with them. Similarly, when we're angry, happy, confused, sad, grateful, hurt, or worried, expressing our needs and emotions to God bonds us to him more closely.

We strengthen our connection to God through prayer. That connection can happen anywhere, at any time. No special equipment is required. There is no dress code, no ticket to purchase, no admission fee. All we need is an open heart. Saint Jeanne Jugan reminds us:

Jesus is waiting for you in the chapel. Go and find him when your strength and patience are giving out, when you feel lonely and helpless. Say to him: 'You know well what is happening, my dear Jesus. I have only you. Come to my aid. ... ' And then go your way. ... It is enough to have told our good Lord.

When we make that prayer connection, we are communicating with God. There are many ways to communicate, and you might find that you don't pray the same way now as you did when you were a child. You might prefer different styles or methods of prayer. Your favorite place to pray can change, as well. And your prayer preferences are most likely different from those of your parents, children, spouse, or friends.

Whether you pray the Rosary at the kitchen table or in the adoration chapel, whether you whisper a prayer for your children as you fold the laundry, whether you begin your day by opening the Bible or end it with Night Prayer from the Liturgy of the Hours, you're praying. You're forging that connection with God. And if you want to (or if your circumstances demand it) you can communicate with God in a different way tomorrow.

As we explore the who, what, where, when, how, and what ifs of praying, my prayer for you is that the connection you are working to build with God will be strong and deep. May you be as open to what he has to say to you as he is to hearing what you express to him.

That is *why* we pray.

Who Should Pray?

Anyone who wishes to deepen their relationship with God should pray. Prayer is not reserved for certain groups or types of people. Anyone — everyone — can pray.

Praying alone

"[Jesus] went up on the mountain by himself to pray" (Mt 14:23).

Solitary prayer provides a very personal opportunity to communicate and connect with God. When you pray alone, you can choose the form of prayer, the length of time you will spend, and the location in which you will pray. I have a comfortable chair in my office, where I often pray in the early mornings. With my computer shut down and a cup of tea by my side, I start the day by praying Morning Prayer from the Liturgy of the Hours, then ponder the day's Mass readings.

Solitary prayer offers an intimate connection with God, and you can find solitude in a variety of places — your car with the radio off, the adoration chapel, a quiet church before or after Mass, or even the laundry room as you match socks.

Praying As a family

"The family that prays together stays together" (Venerable Patrick Peyton).

When you pray as a family, you help your children learn to nurture their own relationships with God and to turn to him in thanksgiving, in need, and in the everyday. If your family does not regularly pray together now, consider beginning with grace before meals. Thank God for the food you are about to receive, ask a blessing on the cook (and the cleanup crew), and commend to God's care any special intentions your family may have.

When my children were small, bedtime

was an important time for family prayer. As we settled our little ones down for the night, we taught the children to recite the Angel of God prayer, followed by a blessing for each family member and a quick thanksgiving for the blessings of the day.

Praying a Rosary or the Divine Mercy Chaplet — or even just a decade of the Rosary — are other ways a family can pray together.

Praying in a group

"Again, [amen,] I say to you, if two of you agree on earth about anything for which they are to pray, it shall be granted to them by my heavenly Father. For where two or three are gathered together in my name, there am I in the midst of them" (Mt 18:19–20).

One of the most beautiful ways to connect with God is when you pray with a group. There is strength in numbers! This is especially true when the group is praying with a common purpose.

Every time you attend Mass, you are

praying as a community. But group prayer doesn't have to be as formal as a Mass. The music director for an ensemble I sing with begins every rehearsal with a prayer: "Thank you, God, for the gift of music and the gift of each other, and for the opportunity to share that gift for your honor and glory."

Whether your group numbers two or three, or hundreds or thousands, uniting in shared prayer can build each person's relationship with God and with others.

Who should pray? *You* should pray.

What Is Prayer?

Prayer is the way we connect with God. It can take many forms, but generally goes in four directions — all of which lead to God. These directions are easy to remember with the acronym ACTS:

- Adoration
- Contrition
- Thanksgiving
- Supplication

The Book of Psalms is a prayer book, right inside the Bible. When you read the psalms or pray them at Mass or in the Liturgy of the Hours, you use the words as old as King David in your prayer. Within the psalms, you can find prayers of all kinds. Similarly, your church hymnal contains examples of each type of prayer. Look to the psalms and hymns as prayer starters.

Adoration, in this sense, just means praising the Lord. Any time you marvel at the wonders of creation or simply praise God's work, you are praying in adoration. Cardinal Robert Sarah explains, "Adoration consists of placing ourselves in the presence of God in an attitude of humility and love." Psalms 62, 95, 100, and 150 are examples of this type of prayer. The traditional hymns "All Hail Adored Trinity" and "All Creatures of Our God and King," along with "Shout to the Lord" by Darlene Joyce Zschech, are songs of praise and adoration.

Contrition is an expression of sorrow for sins and resolution to avoid sin in the future. We pray in contrition at the beginning of Mass during the penitential rite, and we pray the Act of Contrition as part of the Sacrament of Penance. But we can pray with contrition at any time, and we're encouraged to regularly examine our consciences and pray in this way. Psalms 51 and 130 are examples of prayers of repentance, or contrition. Hymns and songs of contrition include the traditional "Softly and Tenderly Jesus is Calling" and "You Alone" by Sarah Hart.

Thanksgiving is prayer of gratitude. Whether you want to thank God for answered prayer or simply offer thanks for the blessings you recognize in your own life, you are thanking and praising God. Each time we pray grace before meals, we pray in thanksgiving. During Mass, the priest calls us: "Let us give thanks to the Lord our God." Many psalms, such as Psalms 16, 92, and 116, are examples of this type of prayer, as are "Now Thank We All Our God" and "Forever" by Chris Tomlin.

Supplication is the kind of prayer in which we ask God for blessings for ourselves or others. That does not mean it's a selfish kind of prayer: Asking God to heal a loved one who is sick or injured, or to help an unemployed friend find meaningful and dignified work, are not selfish requests. Even though we know that God knows what's in our hearts and what's best for us, we can — and should — place our needs before him in prayer. Jesus instructs us to do this in the Sermon on the Mount: "Ask and it will be given to you; seek and you will find; knock and the door will be opened to you" (Mt 7:7). Read Psalms 27, 86, and 102, or sing "Dona Nobis Pacem," "Prayer of Saint Francis" by Sebastian Temple, or "Christ Be Our Light" by Bernadette Farrell.

We can intercede for others by praying for them in supplication — asking God to bless others with what they need. As a Church, we do this during Mass at the prayer of the faithful, when as a community we pray for various needs in the Church, the world, and in our parish and families. We also ask the community to pray for us during the penitential act, and together we enlist the aid of the Blessed Mother, the angels, and the Communion of Saints.

In our private supplication and intercessory prayer, we can also ask the angels and saints to bring our prayers before God. We can use our own words, formal prayers of the Church, or a combination. Just as we ask our family and friends to pray for us in times of crisis or trouble, we can and should enlist the aid of those in heaven who are already close to God.

How Do I Pray?

There are many ways to pray, because there is not just one single way to reach God. Your circumstances, schedule, and inclinations will lead you toward some methods of prayer more than others. You might find that at different times of your life you're attracted to different ways to pray.

The Church offers quite a few formal methods of prayer: these follow a particular format and structure. Informal methods of prayer are also encouraged as private prayer methods. Of all the methods of prayer, though, only one is required by the Church: participation in the Mass.

The Mass

The *Catechism of the Catholic Church* explains that the Mass is "a participation in Christ's own prayer addressed to the Father in the Holy Spirit. In the liturgy, all Christian prayer finds its source and goal" (1073). Participation in Mass is not optional; Mass is not a private devotion but a community prayer, in which all who are assembled are united in praise and thanksgiving to God. While we are encouraged to pray privately before and after Mass, during the liturgy our role is to participate by listening to the readings and homily, proclaiming (or singing, when this is the custom) the responses, and joining our hearts to the intentions of the Church and all assembled for prayer at that time.

At Mass, the Church recalls and re-creates Christ's sacrifice from the Last Supper to his passion and death on the cross. As we pray together at Mass, "the whole community of the faithful encounters the risen Lord who invites them to his banquet" (CCC 1166).

In *Introduction to the Devout Life,* Saint Francis de Sales noted that "prayer made in union with this divine sacrifice has untold power" and calls the Mass "the very center point of our Christian religion." And, as Saint Josemaría Escrivá taught, "we are led to God, brought close to him, by the liturgy of the Catholic Church."

The Liturgy of the Hours

The Liturgy of the Hours, also called the Divine Office, follows a daily rhythm of prayer through the liturgical year. The best-known of the hours are Morning Prayer (also called Lauds), Evening Prayer (Vespers), and Night Prayer (Compline), but there are other hours of prayer during the day. The word "hour" here does not refer to the length of time it takes to pray these prayers; instead, it means that a particular hour is prayed at a certain time of day.

The Liturgy of the Hours is rooted in the monastic tradition and is prayed daily by priests and religious. However, everyone is encouraged to pray this prayer of the Church. It can be prayed in a group — it was originally designed to be prayed in community — or on your own.

If Scripture is inspiring to you and structure is helpful when you pray, the Liturgy of the Hours is a perfect fit. It is rich in Scripture: Based on the Psalms (nearly all the Psalms are included in the full Liturgy of the Hours), each hour also includes readings from the Old and New Testaments and Gospel canticles among the prayers. Everything repeats on a four-week cycle, which is frequent enough that you'll welcome the return of familiar, favorite Psalms and readings, but not so frequent that it becomes boring.

Praying the Liturgy of the Hours also brings the opportunity to learn about and celebrate the saints. You'll find some saints' writings, or essays about particular saints, included among the readings for their feasts. These may lead you to search for spiritual books by and about these saints to incorporate into your prayer in other ways.

Because the Liturgy of the Hours is based on the Church's liturgical calendar and can be complicated to follow, it helps to learn the basics within a group or with a partner, or use an app to read or listen to the prayers.

The Rosary

Meditate on the life of Christ by praying the Rosary. This structured set of prayers, counted out on the familiar string with five groups of ten beads called "decades," commemorates twenty significant events, most of which have a scriptural connection. These events, known as "mysteries," are divided into four sets and are traditionally assigned to certain days of the week.

The Joyful Mysteries
(Monday and Saturday)

- The Annunciation
- The Visitation
- The Birth of Our Lord
- The Presentation in the Temple

- The Finding of the Child Jesus in the Temple

The Sorrowful Mysteries
(Tuesday and Friday)

- The Agony in the Garden
- The Scourging at the Pillar
- The Crowning with Thorns
- The Carrying of the Cross
- The Crucifixion

The Glorious Mysteries
(Wednesday and Sunday)

- The Resurrection
- The Ascension of Our Lord
- The Descent of the Holy Spirit
- The Assumption of Our Lady into Heaven
- The Coronation of the Blessed Virgin Mary

The Mysteries of Light (Thursday)

- The Baptism in the Jordan
- The Wedding at Cana

- The Proclamation of the Kingdom of God
- The Transfiguration
- The Institution of the Eucharist

Venerable Patrick Peyton, who dedicated his priestly ministry to promoting the Rosary, wrote, "The Rosary is not merely a series of prayers to be recited; it is a series of thoughts to be dwelt on, to be turned over in the mind, to be applied in daily life." If you find it difficult to meditate on the mysteries as you pray the Rosary, try reading the reflections on the mysteries in a book about the Rosary or listening to them in an app, audio recording, or podcast. A scriptural Rosary, which associates a particular Scripture verse with each prayer, is another way to focus on the mysteries. Finally, taking a moment before praying each mystery, to envision yourself taking part in that particular episode from the life of Jesus or Mary, can enrich your prayer.

A rosary is easy to carry, so you can pray

it anywhere: in church, at home, in the car, or even in a dentist's chair. If you find that you're often interrupted while praying the Rosary, or struggle to get through the whole thing, pray a decade at a time throughout the day. The tangible rosary beads help you keep count of the prayers, but if you don't have a rosary handy, counting on your fingers is always an option.

Lectio Divina

The practice of *lectio divina* also immerses you in Scripture, but not in the same way as the Rosary. *Lectio divina*, developed in the fourth century and based on the Jewish tradition of telling and retelling the story of the first Passover, includes several readings of the same Scripture passage with a deeper dive into the meaning of the passage each time. If you wish, use a journal to gather your thoughts during each of the four steps of this type of prayer.

At the first step, *lectio*, you read the passage slowly, two or three times. You might even try reading it aloud. As you reread the passage, notice words or phrases that stick out to you. You may notice something different with each reading.

Next, spend some time meditating on the reading. In this step, *meditatio,* you'll reflect on the full passage, line by line. This is prayer, not study, so you're focusing on the message God has for you in this reading.

The third step, *oratio,* is your response to God's message for you. Pray about what this message makes you feel; ask God for guidance if you feel called to action.

End by contemplating silently. This last step, *contemplatio,* is a time to rest and allow God's message to settle into your soul. If you find yourself distracted during this time, gently gather your attention again, perhaps by repeating a word or phrase from the Scripture you have been reading.

Allow enough time so that you don't have to rush through the steps. Some parts of the process may take longer than others.

Novenas

Novenas are an exercise of perseverance in prayer. Generally, a novena is a set of prayers that is prayed for nine consecutive days, or sometimes on a particular day of the week for nine consecutive weeks. We pray novenas with a special intention in mind.

Often, novenas begin nine days before a saint's feast day or other feast of the Church — for example, a novena to the Holy Spirit generally begins nine days before Pentecost. But a novena can be prayed at any time for any reason.

Novenas involve repeating the same prayer or set of prayers for the nine days, sometimes with small changes of intention or focus. For example, to pray the Divine Mercy novena, which begins on Good Friday and ends on Divine Mercy Sunday, you pray the Divine Mercy Chaplet on each of the nine days. Each day is assigned a specific prayer intention.

For the sick, pray the novena to Our Lady of Lourdes. The novena to Our Lady of

Fátima is a prayer for peace and conversion of sinners. You can pray the novena to Saint Joseph for fathers, for employment, or if you want to sell your house. If you believe your situation is an impossible cause, pray the novena to Saint Jude the Apostle or Saint Rita of Cascia.

If your prayer intention is time-sensitive and you don't have nine days for a full novena, try Saint Teresa of Calcutta's Express Novena (sometimes called a Flying Novena). Simply pray nine Memorares for your intention and then a tenth Memorare in thanksgiving for an answer to your prayer. (Yes, you are thanking God in advance!) You can pray this novena on the go, because you only need to know the words to one prayer to complete it.

The parable of the persistent widow, recounted in Luke 18:1–8, underscores the importance of persevering in prayer. Sticking to a novena for nine full days shows that you are dedicated to praying for your special intention.

Other Prayers of the Church

The Angelus, a short prayer based on the account of the Annunciation in the Gospel of Luke, can be prayed on your own or in a group. Typically prayed three times a day — 9 a.m., noon, and 6 p.m. — the Angelus is easy to learn and can be prayed anywhere. (You might recognize the closing prayer of the Angelus — it is often used to end a recitation of the Rosary.)

Chaplets offer your hands something to do while you pray and involve patterns of repeated prayers. The best-known chaplet is the Rosary, but Catholic tradition includes many other chaplets for a variety of special intentions. Some of these, such as the Divine Mercy Chaplet, can be prayed on a traditional rosary. Others, not based on five sets of ten prayers, require a different set of beads and, usually, different prayers. If you have a devotion to Saint Michael the Archangel, Saint Joseph, Saint Anne, Saint Andrew, or the Five Wounds of Jesus, you can find a chaplet to express that devotion. You can also pray a variety of chaplets with a connection to the Blessed Mother. The seven-decade Franciscan Crown, similar to the Rosary, commemorates the Seven Joys of Mary, and other chaplets are dedicated to the Immaculate Conception, the Immaculate Heart of Mary, Our Lady Star of the Sea, and the Seven Sorrows of Mary.

How Do I Pray
on My Own?

The prayers of the Church are formal prayers, following a certain format or structure. But you don't always need or want to use someone else's words to tell God what's in your heart. You can pray on your own in a variety of ways.

Before the Blessed Sacrament

Try spending time in a church or adoration chapel praying in the presence of the Blessed Sacrament. You can make a full holy hour or simply stop by for a visit. My dad used to take us kids into an empty church on occasion, telling us that we were going in "to say hi to God." That was an encouragement to use our own words in prayer.

Meditation

Quieting your mind and heart in meditation allows you to listen for God's voice in prayer: "We pass from thoughts to reality. To the extent that we are humble and faithful, we discover in meditation the movements that stir the heart and we are able to discern them. It is a question of asking truthfully in order to come into the light: 'Lord, what do you want me to do?'" (CCC 2706).

For a guided meditation experience, look for Catholic apps with audio prompts to get started. Meditation is often part of other types of prayer, including the Rosary and *lectio divina*. You can meditate upon Scripture, events in the life of Christ, or spiritual reading. Use any of these as a jumping-off point for prayer.

Spiritual reading

Opening a spiritual book, whether it is the Bible, a devotional book, or the writings of a saint, can be an excellent gateway to prayer. Spiritual reading, though, is not the same as studying. The object is not to reach the end of the book and understand everything in it. Reading even a sentence or two can light a prayerful spark. Keep a journal by your side to record your reflections.

Creative pursuits

I've been a musician at church since I was a teenager, so making music has always been an integral part of the way I pray. Whether I'm participating in a musical ensemble for Mass or concerts, singing along to praise music in the car, or playing and singing hymns on my own that reflect what I want to say to God in that moment, making music has become a prayer for me.

Even if you don't play an instrument and don't think you can sing, you can still appreciate the role of music in prayer. Meditate on the lyrics of a favorite hymn or song of praise. Listening to Scripture-based music is an innovative way to begin to pray with the Scriptures.

Using your hands to create art can also

bring your mind to prayer. Painting religious images such as the Nativity or the Sacred Heart, photographing God's glory evident in nature's beauty, forming a sculpture out of clay, or using calligraphy to write out a quote from Scripture or a saint are all gateways to prayer — and, like music, can be gateways to pray with others.

Writing poetry and journaling allow you to use words in prayer in creative ways. Simply scribble down your hopes, dreams, questions, and struggles. Turn off your inner editor; this doesn't need to be perfect. As you write, you may discover that God is gently leading you to a resolution, solution, or course of action.

Offering it up

Turn any struggle, inconvenience, or difficulty into a prayer by offering it up to benefit someone else. Saint Paul sums up the concept in his Letter to the Colossians: "Now I rejoice in my sufferings for your sake, and in my flesh I am filling up what is lacking in the afflictions of Christ on behalf of his body, which is the church" (1:24).

You can always offer up any suffering, great or small, for the sake of the souls in purgatory. But you can also offer it up much closer to home. I have promised to offer up the pain from tennis elbow for a friend of mine who recently had surgery for a more severe form of the same condition. When I was woken up in the wee hours of the morning to aid my youngest child, who has diabetes, I'd offer the resulting exhaustion for other parents of children with diabetes who were also struggling with difficult nights. In this way, you turn your pain into someone else's gain. You turn your pain into a prayer.

What Do the Scriptures and the Saints Tell Us about Prayer?

The Scriptures

The Scriptures are full of lessons about prayer, including the ultimate lesson in prayer, Matthew 6:9–13, when Jesus specifically tells us how to pray by giving us the words to the Lord's Prayer. He exhorts also, "Love your enemies, and pray for those who persecute you" (Mt 5:44).

Saint Paul frequently wrote about prayer, encouraging his audience to pray at all times: "With all prayer and supplication, pray at every opportunity in the Spirit. To that end, be watchful with all perseverance and supplication for all the holy ones" (Eph 6:18); and, "Have no anxiety at all, but in everything, by prayer and petition, with thanksgiving, make your requests known to God" (Phil 4:6).

Saint James expands on Paul's advice, detailing some situations that call for prayer:

> Is anyone among you suffering? He should pray. Is anyone in good spirits? He should sing praise. Is anyone among you sick? He should summon the presbyters of the church, and they should pray over him and anoint [him] with oil in the name of the Lord, and the prayer of faith will save the sick person, and the Lord will raise him up. If he has committed any sins, he will be forgiven. (James 5:13–15)

Saint Paul encourages those who experience difficulty praying more than once, explaining that we should let the Holy Spirit take over: "The Spirit too comes to the aid of our weakness; for we do not know how to pray as we ought, but the Spirit itself intercedes with inexpressible groanings" (Rom 8:26). "Rejoice in hope, endure in affliction, persevere in prayer" (Rom 12:12) is the centerpiece of Saint Paul's instructions to the faithful.

The Psalms, essentially prayers themselves, also offer observations about prayer: "The LORD is near to all who call upon him, / to all who call upon him in truth" (Ps 145:18). The prophet Jeremiah echoes this as he repeats a message from God: "When you call me, and come and pray to me, I will listen to you" (Jer 29:12). This message is echoed in the First Letter of John: "And we have this confidence in him, that if we ask anything according to his will, he hears us. And if we know that he hears us in regard to whatever we ask, we know that what we have asked him for is ours" (1 Jn 5:14–15).

The Saints

The saints, as well, offer lessons about prayer and encouragement to pray. "In prayer we speak with God and hear him," Saint Francis of Assisi observed. This saint frequently followed Jesus' example of going off alone to pray and deeply believed in the importance of staying connected with God.

A good portion of Saint Francis de Sales' *Introduction to the Devout Life* concerns prayer. This spiritual classic, originally written as letters to a relative who was under his spiritual direction, emphasizes the beauty of prayer and the importance of setting time apart for communication with God: "If we cling to the Savior in meditation, listening to his words, watching his actions and intentions, we will learn in time, through his grace, to speak, act, and will like him. … There is no way to God except through this door."

Saint Thérèse of Lisieux's simple approach to prayer mirrors her humble Little Way: "I have not the courage to look through books for beautiful prayers. … I do as children who have not learned to read — I simply tell Our Lord all that I want, and he always understands." The saint's words are comforting to those who fear that prayer must be complicated or that they must follow an unfamiliar, uncomfortable format.

Saint John Henry Newman preached that prayer is essential: "Prayer is to spiritual life what the beating of the pulse and the drawing of the breath are to the life of the body." In the same sermon, he defined prayer as, "What is prayer but the expression, the voice, of faith?"

Venerable Patrick Peyton, who devoted his priestly ministry to encouraging family prayer, proclaimed, "The family that prays together stays together" and "A world at prayer is a world at peace." Father Peyton noted in his autobiography that his dedication to this work began during his days as a seminarian during World War II: "What was needed was not simply an end to the fighting but an atmosphere of true peace, peace in the heart, peace in the home, peace in the family." His work stemmed from his deep belief in the power of prayer to change hearts.

When Should I Pray?

Saint Paul calls us to "pray without ceasing" in his First Letter to the Thessalonians (see 5:17). Your prayer times can be scheduled (formal) or spontaneous, and by combining the two you'll achieve that goal of praying at all times.

The Church offers many occasions for scheduled prayer. The most obvious, and most important, is the Mass. This is a dedicated time when the community comes together in prayer and sacrifice, as we were called to do so by Jesus at the Last Supper.

Eucharistic Adoration, also known as a Holy Hour, is another formal prayer occasion. If a parish has Perpetual Adoration of the Eucharist, adorers must follow a schedule to ensure that there is always someone present when the Body of Christ is exposed in the church or chapel. Other parishes may have specific days or times for Adoration.

The Liturgy of the Hours, also called the Divine Office, is the daily prayer of the Church. Several times a day, the faithful are called to prayer: morning, daytime, evening, and night; there is also an Office of Readings that is generally prayed before Morning Prayer. In praying the Liturgy of the Hours, you will encounter nearly all of the psalms, and often you will notice the correlation between the words of a particular psalm and the time of day it is to be prayed. We can begin and end our days with the Liturgy of the Hours, sanctifying the different times of day with the same prayers that are used by Catholic priests, religious, deacons, and lay people throughout the world.

The Angelus is traditionally prayed in the morning, at noon, and in the evening. Short and simple to memorize, the Angelus can be prayed without special books and was intended to be prayed anywhere. When you pray the Angelus, you honor the Blessed Mother's fiat and ask her to intercede for you on your path to holiness. The prayer originated in the Middle Ages as a practice for lay people and mirrored the monastic tradition of praying the Liturgy of the Hours. Church bells would often be used as calls to prayer, so that the faithful would pause in their work and take a moment to pray. Consider setting an alarm on your phone or smart watch to remind you to pray the Angelus as you begin and end work, and break for lunch.

Finally, mealtime can become an opportunity for prayer when you begin the meal with a prayer of thanksgiving (grace before meals).

Spontaneous prayer, on the other hand, can take place at any time. Such prayer can be short aspirations such as "Jesus, I trust in you" or even "God, help me," or longer periods of prayer and meditation. Before and after Mass, if your schedule and circumstances permit, try taking a few moments to pray in the church. Doing so before Mass will help you prepare spiritually for the Mass; after Mass, offer your thanksgiving to God before going about your day.

If someone asks you to pray for them, pray right away. Don't wait! Then, promise to continue to remember their intention in prayer in a concrete way or at a certain time. It's important to follow through on promises of prayer.

Consider some ways to add spontaneous, informal prayer to your day. You might already do these things:

- Begin the day with a prayer of thanksgiving to God for another day.
- As you begin your work, schoolwork, or household chores, ask God to bless your efforts and the people they impact.
- Use moments and transitions in your day as prayer cues. Offer a short prayer when you get into the car, when the phone

rings, or when you shift gears to begin a new type of task.

- If you happen to pass an adoration chapel in the course of your day, take a moment to stop in and offer a quick prayer in the presence of the Blessed Sacrament.

- End the day with an Act of Contrition, seeking pardon for the ways you haven't lived up to what God calls you to do.

When can you pray? Any time: the beginning, middle, or end of the day!

Where Should I Pray?

In the same way that prayer can be a formal or informal experience, and just as you can use your own words to pray or draw upon Scripture and the prayers of the Church, the where of prayer, with one notable exception, is up to you.

That exception is, of course, the Mass. Under most circumstances, Mass must take place in a church, chapel, cathedral, or basilica. A church is a dedicated space for prayer. Even if Mass is not happening at a given time, a church is set aside for prayer and worship. The Blessed Sacrament is nearly always present in a church, so it is a place where you can pray in the presence of Jesus in the Eucharist.

An adoration chapel is another such

place: a prayer space set apart where you can spend time with Jesus — Body, Blood, Soul, and Divinity. It is a place of reverent silence where you can quiet your soul and listen to God. Adoration chapels are open to anyone, but adorers often come and go for scheduled Holy Hours to ensure that the Blessed Sacrament is never left alone in the chapel.

While few people have room in their homes for an actual chapel, anyone can carve out a little prayer area by bringing together a crucifix, some religious art, and perhaps a candle, a Rosary, and your favorite prayer book. A corner, shelf, or mantel is enough room for the essentials to create an atmosphere dedicated to prayer.

You can find prayer spaces outside your home or church as well. Many churches and shrines offer outdoor prayer spaces such as Rosary gardens or outdoor Stations of the Cross. These invite people of faith to step away from their busy lives for a few moments and engage in prayer in a beautiful, peaceful place.

But prayer can happen anywhere: at your kitchen sink, as you scrub the dinner dishes; in your favorite chair with a cup of tea by your side; on your porch steps; at the bedside of an ailing loved one. For me, it's often my car, if I'm alone and driving some distance. I turn off the radio and turn over my thoughts to God.

Why do you need to go to Mass if you can pray anywhere? The Mass is more than simply community prayer to which the Church calls all who are able to participate. At Mass, we take part in the re-creation of the mysteries of our salvation, joining together in the central prayer of our faith.

That doesn't take anything away from the time you spend in prayer on the beach at sunrise or as stars sparkle in the sky outside your window. But private prayer and Mass are not the same, and we are called to mark the Sabbath Day by attending Mass. Our community prayer at Mass and reception of the sacraments enrich and inspire our personal times of prayer.

Where can you pray? You can pray anywhere.

What If ... ?

What if I get distracted?

Distraction is inevitable. It doesn't mean you're not holy; it simply means you're human. You have a lot going on in your life, and you can't turn off your thoughts, concerns, worries, and plans like a faucet when it's time to pray.

The *Catechism of the Catholic Church* notes that prayer is a battle — it requires effort (see 2725). Distraction is definitely a factor in that battle, and it even happened to the saints.

Saint Thérèse of Lisieux offered advice to a fellow Carmelite who struggled with distractions in prayer: "As soon as I am aware of them, I pray for those people the thought of whom is diverting my attention, and in this way they reap benefit from my distractions. I accept all for the love of God, even the wildest fancies that cross my mind."

Listing your distractions in a prayer journal can help you bring them to prayer. Just as writing down the to-do list that's swirling around in your brain and keeping you from falling asleep works to settle your mind late at night, journaling those distracting thoughts and bringing them to God can calm your spirit and allow you to enter into deeper prayer.

This strategy of turning a distraction into an opportunity for prayer can be very effective, especially if you're trying to pray in an environment that doesn't allow for silence or often includes interruptions.

A teacher's call to action, "Quiet on the outside, quiet on the inside" sums up another technique to beat distraction. Listen to sacred music or plug your earbuds in to some white noise to create a calm atmosphere. Close your eyes — or open them: focus your vision on a crucifix or religious art. Still your busy hands by praying a Rosary.

What if I don't feel anything?

There will be plenty of times when you pray — yet feel nothing.

It's discouraging. You go to God in prayer and you hope — you expect — that you'll get an answer immediately. You ask, seek, and knock, but nothing seems different.

Are you doing something wrong? Is your prayer good enough?

It's never wrong to bring your concerns to God in prayer. You're right to share what's on your heart with him. But God's way of receiving our prayer is different from our way of offering it.

When you pray but feel nothing, that does not mean that God didn't hear you. It doesn't mean that your prayer didn't check the right boxes on God's list. It doesn't mean that your prayer was not (or will not be) answered. There is much more to prayer than your emotional response.

Many saints have written about the experience of spiritual dryness. Saint Ignatius of Loyola used the term "desolation" to describe those times when prayer seemed unfulfilling. *Dark Night of the Soul*, a spiritual classic by Saint John of the Cross, describes that saint's suffering and struggle.

Saint Thérèse of Lisieux details her own state of spiritual dryness at the beginning of Chapter VIII of *Story of a Soul*, blaming it on her lack of fidelity and her habit of falling asleep during her meditation time. Mother Teresa soldiered through decades of spiritual darkness, even as she ministered to the dying poor and took on the most humble of tasks.

If you don't feel anything, you're not alone. The saints who have been there and done that agree that when you're in a time of spiritual dryness, you should persevere. Pray anyway. Don't let the darkness steal your motivation.

What if I don't feel like praying?

Everyone has times when they just don't feel like praying. But just as we should go to work or school even though we might no feel like it, and just as we should eat nutritious food and go to bed earlier when it's easy to find excuses not to do those things, we need to pray anyway. If your prayer time rolls around and you're just not feeling it, the best thing you can do is fight the temptation to give up. The issue truly is one of temptation. Try one of these five strategies for fighting that feeling:

1. Ask God to help you want to pray.
2. Pray anyway — but try something different. Change your prayer routine, location, or method, or get inspired by reading a new spiritual book.
3. Start slowly. Begin by listening to music, reading a psalm, or even journaling. Write a letter to God about whatever's steal-

ing your motivation to pray.
Doing that is a prayer!

4. Settle in. If your mind is racing
    in several different directions,
    a repetitive prayer like the
    Rosary or the Divine Mercy
    Chaplet can help quiet your
    thoughts.

5. Ask for help. Pray for the in-
    tercession of Saint Michael the
    Archangel to help you battle
    that temptation to slack off in
    prayer.

What if I don't get an answer?

An answered prayer is not the same as a
granted wish. The Bible is full of stories of
people who prayed fervently. Some received
immediate answers to their prayer. Others
waited a very long time. Most of them were
not answered as was expected or wished. But
all of them were answered.

When he showed us the way to pray, Jesus emphasized that we are to say, "Thy will

be done." He did this himself in the Garden of Gethsemane when he prayed that the Father would take away the suffering Jesus knew he was about to endure. Yet after pouring out his heart to God, Jesus surrendered to the will of his Father.

Jesus never promised to grant our wishes. He did promise that God would give us what is good for us:

> Which one of you would hand his son a stone when he asks for a loaf of bread, or a snake when he asks for a fish? If you then, who are wicked, know how to give good gifts to your children, how much more will your heavenly Father give good things to those who ask him. (Matthew 7:9–11)

If you bring your wish list to God and expect him to give you everything you want, you will be disappointed. That doesn't mean you shouldn't bring your wish list to God. Tell him what is on your heart. Tell him what you hope for. Tell him your dreams — big ones and little ones.

You will always get an answer. It will not always be the answer you want, but God knows what you need.

What if I try a prayer method but it doesn't "work" for me?

There is only one prayer that Catholics are required to participate in: the Mass. You might not feel like you are getting anything out of it, but there is grace in the presence of the Sacrament and in your obedience to the obligation to attend Mass on Sundays and holy days of obligation. There are ways to improve your own prayer at Mass: Preparing ahead of time by reading and praying about the Scriptures for the day, and building in a little extra time so you're not rushed as you arrive at church, will help you pray better at Mass. Bringing a prayer card to read after you receive Communion will focus your attention on the Sacrament.

Besides Mass, Catholics are called to pray, but the details are up to each individual. Priests, deacons, and religious are required to pray the Liturgy of the Hours, and in some cases the Rosary and other prayers are included in their spiritual discipline. But most Catholics are completely on their own when it comes to deciding how they will pray.

What works for you at one time in your life might not work at another. If your current state in life does not require a particular spiritual practice, and you find that it is not fruitful for you, try something different. Don't stop completely; shift gears instead. Make a small change, such as adding music in the background or sitting in a different seat.

Or make a large change. Try a prayer practice for a period of time to see what works for you. A novena takes only nine days. In October, traditionally the month of the Rosary, pray the Rosary; during Lent, pray the Stations of the Cross; in Advent, light the candles of your Advent wreath and read through the book of the prophet Isaiah.

Find the way you like best to pray, and don't be afraid to try something new.

What if I'm so stressed out I can't focus?

It happens to all of us. The pressures and worries and deadlines and concerns of our lives consume all our energies, including the energy we want to channel into prayer. We feel as if we just can't concentrate on one more thing.

It's okay to give that to God as your prayer. I have found that until I do exactly that, I can't find another way to pray. But God can take it. In fact, he already has — just look at a crucifix for proof.

Ask for God's help in turning your cares over to him. "Cast all your worries upon him because he cares for you" (1 Pt 5:7). You can name your worries one by one, or just hand over the whole pile at once. Admitting that you can't do it on your own is probably the best prayer you can pray in that moment.

This is also a time when formal prayers can be comforting. Praying a Rosary or Divine Mercy Chaplet can help you slow your thoughts and find room to breathe in your pain.

When you have a lot on your plate, keep it simple, and hand it over to God.

What if I forget to pray?

There's absolutely nothing wrong with needing a reminder to pray — and that need is nothing new. That's why the Angelus bells were rung: to remind the faithful to pause and pray at certain times throughout their day.

Most of us don't live or work in places where we can hear church bells, but we have many other options for personal prayer reminders. I like to find creative ways to remind myself to pray.

I'm in the middle of a novena as I write this, and the only reason I've even made it to day seven is that I set a prayer appointment at noon each day in my Google calendar. When

I see that notification pop up, I stop what I'm doing and pray the novena. Many of my friends set alarms in their smartphones to pray the Divine Mercy Chaplet at 3:00 p.m.

You don't need technology to act as your prayer reminder, though. My favorite reminders are all around me. When I use that coffee mug my older son gave me, I can offer a prayer for him. When I drive or walk past the street where my friend lives, I can pray for that friend.

Because I notice cars, I decided to turn that into a prayer reminder. A black sedan in front of me on the road is a cue to pray for my husband. Magnets or decals advertising colleges or vacation destinations that I associate with family members or friends remind me to pray for those people. I've been known to ask faraway friends or relatives what kind of car they're driving now, so I can hold them in my prayers when I see cars like theirs.

Anything that makes you think of a person can be turned into a reminder to pray for that person!

I also like to place little saint statues where I'll see them, with a Post-It Note nearby, with the name of someone for whom I've promised to pray. The trick is to regularly rotate this display so it will catch my eye.

Using prayer reminders in creative ways helps us reach the goal of praying constantly.

What if my go-to prayer methods aren't available?

During the coronavirus pandemic in 2020, churches canceled public Masses in favor of livestreamed liturgy, and adoration chapels closed. In many locations around the world, church buildings closed to the public entirely for several weeks. The faithful were excused from the Sunday Mass obligation even after churches reopened.

Other emergencies, too, can limit options when it comes to prayer practices. When a family emergency required quite a bit of travel, for example, I was unable to attend daily Mass and needed to secure a substitute to cover my weekly holy hour in the adoration chapel.

At times like these, we need to do the best we can with what we have. Pope Francis encouraged Catholics to pray the Rosary during the pandemic. Creative uses of technology allowed people to pray as part of a group, even while quarantined at home. Mass and even Eucharistic Adoration could be found on livestream.

When I needed to help my family and could not attend daily Mass, I could still pray the Rosary and listen to praise music during my long drives. I could still pray the Liturgy of the Hours in the morning and evening. I could still read and pray over the Mass readings each day.

When circumstances close a particular prayer option for you, prayer is still an option.

Final Thoughts

Saint Josemaría Escrivá wrote: "To pray is to talk with God. But about what? ... About him, and yourself: joys, sorrows, successes and failures, great ambitions, daily worries — even your weaknesses! And acts of thanksgiving and petitions — and love and reparation. In short, to get to know him and to get to know yourself."

Prayer doesn't have to be complicated. Ask, seek, and knock. Give glory to God and share what's in your heart.

About the Author

Barb Szyszkiewicz is a wife, mom of three young adults, and a Secular Franciscan. She is editor at CatholicMom.com and blogs at FranciscanMom.com. Barb enjoys writing, cooking, and reading, and is a music minister at her parish.